COME WALK WITH ME

COME WALK WITH ME

AN INVITATION FROM GOD

DAVID HEUTHE

Copyright © 2022 by David Heuthe.

Library of Congress Control Number: 2022921838
ISBN: Hardcover   978-1-6698-5686-3
          Softcover   978-1-6698-5685-6
          eBook   978-1-6698-5687-0

All rights reserved. No part of this book may be reproduced or transmitted in any form or by any means, electronic or mechanical, including photocopying, recording, or by any information storage and retrieval system, without permission in writing from the copyright owner.

Any people depicted in stock imagery provided by Getty Images are models, and such images are being used for illustrative purposes only. Certain stock imagery © Getty Images.

Print information available on the last page.

Rev. date: 11/30/2022

To order additional copies of this book, contact:
Xlibris
844-714-8691
www.Xlibris.com
Orders@Xlibris.com
848445

TO TRICIA MY WIFE OF 40+ YEARS WHO'S ALWAYS SUPPORTED ME. YOU'RE STILL THE ONE.

DEAR READER

THANK YOU FOR TAKING THE TIME TO PURCHASE AND READ MY BOOK. MY HOPE IS THAT IT WILL INSPIRE, ENCOURAGE AND COMFORT YOU IN READING AS MUCH AS IT HAS FOR ME IN WRITING IT. THE BOOK CONTAINS 31 POEMS IN 4 SECTIONS. YOU CAN READ THEM IN THAT ORDER BUT FEEL FREE TO PICK AND CHOOSE IF YOU FIND SOME THAT SPEAK TO YOUR HEART. MY PRAYER IS THAT THESE POEMS WILL HELP YOU SEE GOD AS THE ONE THAT KNOWS YOU BEST AND LOVES YOU MOST.

IN CHRIST,

DAVID HEUTHE

CONTENTS

THE INVITATION

WALK WITH ME	1
WHY DO YOU HIDE	3
BEAUTY OF THE GOSPEL	5
HE'S THE ONE	7
MERCY AND GRACE	9
OPEN GATE	11
TOO MUCH FOR ME	13
LITTLE LAMB	15
WATER INTO WINE	17
LIGHT FROM DARK	19
LIGHTNING AND THUNDER	21
CHILDREN'S SONGS	23

THE FAMILY

FAMILY PRAYER	27
MY ETERNAL FAMILY	31
FAMILY AT HOME	33
HOW TO BAKE	35
WHY	37
ON MY OWN	39
NIGHT SONG	41
REALITY	43
I AM	45

LIKE MY SAVIOR 47

THE BATTLE

COME SONS 51
MOUNTAIN TOP VIEW 53
SON OF MINE 55
I WILL NOT YIELD 57
POWER LOVE 59

THE VICTORY

WHEN THE RACE IS RUN 63
WHAT WILL WE SEE 65
HEAVENLY CROWN 67

THE INVITATION

WALK WITH ME

WALK WITH ME AND YOU WILL HEAR
OF YOU MY SON WHO I LOVE SO DEAR
INSTEAD OF RUNNING HERE AND THERE
LET ME WHISPER IN YOUR EAR

YOUR MIND KNOWS TRUTHS BEYOND ITS BREADTH
BECAUSE IT TAKES THE SPIRITS BREATH
TO PLANT THESE TRUTHS OF WHO YOU ARE
DEEP WITHIN TO HEAL THE SCAR

FOR MANY YEARS YOU'VE SOUGHT TO KNOW
THE HIDDEN THINGS THAT MAKE YOU GO
I HAVE THE ANSWER THAT YOU SEEK
YOU WILL FIND THEM HERE IN ME

I FASHIONED YOU WITH MY OWN HANDS
INSIDE AND OUT, I HAVE A PLAN
BUT BECAUSE I MADE AND LOVE YOU SO
WITHOUT ME YOU CANNOT GO

YOU AND I FIT LIKE HAND AND GLOVE
TOGETHER WITH GUIDANCE FROM ABOVE
ABILITIES BEYOND WHAT YOU CAN DO
WILL FLOW WITH EASE TO YOUR DELIGHT

YOU'VE FELT IT IN THE PAST I KNOW
I'VE SEEN THE JOY, YOU SEEM TO GLOW
I ALSO FEEL THAT JOY, YOU SEE
MY GOAL IS TO HAVE YOU HERE WITH ME

SO WHEN ON STAGE OR DIGGING DITCH
OR RESTING BY A SHADY TREE
IT'S JUST ME AND YOU
COME WALK WITH ME

WHY DO YOU HIDE

WHY DO YOU HIDE IN TROUBLED TIMES
THE LORD GOD SAID TO ME
I'M HERE TO GIVE YOU HELP AND AID
BUT YOU GO WATCH TV

WHAT COULD I SAY IN RESPONSE
IT TRULY MADE NO SENSE
TO PRETEND THAT ALL IS WELL
WHEN IN GREAT DISTRESS

SO I TURNED AROUND
AND TOOK MY TROUBLES TO THE ONE WHO CARES
AND FOUND TO MY GREAT SURPRISE
HE WAS WAITING THERE

HE TOOK MY TROUBLES IN HIS HANDS
AND SPOKE KIND WORDS TO ME
AND IN THE END I REALISED
THAT'S WHERE I WANT TO BE

BEAUTY OF THE GOSPEL

THE BEAUTY OF THE GOSPEL
ALWAYS BRINGS A TEAR
BRINGING PEACE AND HEALING
TO HEARTS ONCE BOUND BY FEAR

THE BEAUTY OF THE GOSPEL
TO THOSE WHO'VE EYES TO SEE
DAZZLE, AMAZE AND TRANSFORM
THE HARDEST HEARTS OF MAN

THE BEAUTY OF THE GOSPEL
IS THE RESTORATION THAT IT BRINGS
FROM A GOD OF LOVE AND MERCY
TO A CREATURE STUCK IN SIN

THE BEAUTY OF THE GOSPEL
IT TAKES OUR SIN AND SHAME
AND PLUNGES THEM BENEATH THE WAVES
NEVER TO RISE AGAIN

THE BEAUTY OF THE GOSPEL
IS THAT A SINNER SUCH AS I
CAN KNOW THIS LOVING GOD
RIGHT NOW AND ETERNALLY

HE'S THE ONE

HE'S THE ONE WHO GAVE HIS ALL
LEFT HIS THRONE TO SAVE MAN'S SOUL
GAVE UP GLORY, POWER OVER ALL
FOR A MANGER IN A STALL

THIS ONE WHO CREATED ALL WE SEE
WALKED DUSTY ROADS TO SET MEN FREE
STILL HE HAD AUTHORITY
TO HEAL THE LAME AND MAKE BLIND MEN SEE

TILL AT LAST HE REACHED HIS GOAL
THE PAINFUL TREE TO SAVE MAN'S SOUL
PAIN WITHOUT AND WITHIN
HE PAID THE PRICE FOR OUR SIN

DEATH DEFEATED HE ROSE TO LIFE
HE ROSE VICTORIOUS IN THE FIGHT
NOW IN THE GLORY HE HAS EARNED
JESUS GOD/ MAN ON THE THRONE

MERCY AND GRACE

MERCY LIKE SWORD
CUTS DOWN VINES OF SHAME
THE LEAVES OF ACCUSATION
THAT CAUSES SO MUCH PAIN

MERCY LIKE A RIVER
CLEANSES HEART AND SOUL
WASHING WASTE AND GARBAGE
MAKING SINNERS WHOLE

GRACE COMES LIKE A BUILDER
MAKING SOMETHING NEW
I KNOW I DON'T DESERVE IT
ALL GLORY GOES TO YOU

GRACE TAKES A BUILDING
MOST PEOPLE WOULD CONDEMN
AND SEES A STATELY MANSION
WITH GARDENS ALL AROUND

MEN AND ANGELS MARVEL
AT THE BUILDING ONCE CONDEMNED
THE NEW PRIDE OF THE NEIGHBORHOOD
THEY'VE FORGOTTEN WHAT HAD BEEN

GRACE AND MERCY MEET AND JOIN
IN A MIGHTY KISS
AND I'M RIGHT IN THE MIDDLE
CRYING BLESSED, BLESSED, BLESSED

OPEN GATE

THE GATE IS OPEN THE TOLL'S BEEN PAID
DOOR'S OPEN WIDE THE PATH IS LAID
THE KEY'S BEEN TURNED, DOOR OPEN WIDE
WHY DO YOU LINGER COME INSIDE

LEAVE YOUR BURDENS AT THE DOOR
THERE'S LIFE INSIDE AND SO MUCH MORE
THE TABLE'S LAID, DELICIOUS FARE
BUT MORE THAN THAT I AM HERE

TOO MUCH FOR ME

TOO MUCH FOR ME TO UNDERSTAND
THE ONE WHO MADE IT WITH HIS HAND
WOULD STOP AT ONCE TO HEAR MY PRAYER
OR IN A BOTTLE STORE MY TEAR

THE VOICE THAT SPOKE AND MADE IT ALL
COULD ALSO SPEAK TO ONE SO SMALL
TO BRING COMFORT TO A HEART
THAT'S BROKEN, SCARED OF THE DARK

SO FEAR NOT MY LITTLE CHILD
THE MIGHTY CREATOR IS ALWAYS NEAR
ALWAYS THERE TO FIGHT THE FIGHT
TRUST IN HIM, IT WILL BE ALRIGHT

LITTLE LAMB

LITTLE LAMB ON THE LAND
TAKE THE TREAT FROM MY HAND
DO NOT TURN IN AWAY IN FEAR
YOU ARE SAFE WHEN I AM NEAR

LOOK TO ME I AM THE ONE
I MADE THE WATER, GRASS AND SUN
I AM THE SOURCE I'M ALL YOU NEED
LISTEN CLOSE MY WORDS WILL FEED

REST AND COMFORT I HAVE FOR YOU
STRENGTH AND JOY AND HEALING TOO
YOU'VE TRIED YOURSELF AND FOUND DISTRESS
COME TO ME AND FIND TRUE REST

WATER INTO WINE

WATER INTO WINE,
OLD LIFE INTO NEW
ONCE DRY AND BARREN
NOW LOVE AND JOY ABOUNDS

PRISONER INTO SON
OUTCAST TO BELOVED
ONCE IN CHAINS AND BONDAGE
SET FREE IN FATHER'S LOVE

ONCE A HOMELESS BEGGAR
NO PLACE TO CALL HIS OWN
ADOPTED BY A LOVING GOD
AND WELCOMED IN HIS HOME

NOW I SIT AT TABLE SET
MY NAME DENOTES MY PLACE
A LAVISH FARE I DON'T DESERVE
I OWN BY GOD'S GOOD GRACE

LIGHT FROM DARK

LIGHT FROM DARK HOW CAN IT BE
A PRISONER ONCE NOW SET FREE
BEYOND THE BARS I SAW A LIGHT
IN THE DISTANCE VERY BRIGHT

ONCE I THOUGHT I COULD SEE
BLINDED BY THE PRIDE IN ME
BUT STRUCK BROUGHT LOW BY PIERCING LIGHT
FINALLY I LOST THE WILL TO FIGHT

WHEN ALL WAS DONE THE FIGHT IN VAIN
I CRIED "WHO WILL SAVE ME FROM THIS PAIN"
COME WITH ME I HEARD HIM SAY
FLOW ME NEW LIFE YOU'LL GAIN

MY FOE IS NOW MY GREAT REWARD
THE ONE I FOUGHT IS NOW MY LORD
WITH SURRENDER I FOUND PEACE
INSTEAD OF PAIN SWEET RELEASE

LIGHTNING AND THUNDER

LIGHTNING AND THUNDER, SINGING BIRDS
WIND AND RAIN THE OCEAN SURGE
COLORED FLOWERS SCENTED SWEET
YELLOW SAND BLUE OCEAN MEET

FROM VAST SKY TO SMALLEST CELL
COMPLICATED BUT WORKS SO WELL
THE PLANETS AND STARS FLUNG FROM YOUR HAND
AND WITH THE SAME YOU FORMED MAN

BY YOUR WORD YOU MADE IT ALL
WITHOUT YOU IT ALL WOULD FALL
THE UNIVERSE SO GREAT AND GRAND
WOULD SOON DISSOLVE WITHOUT YOUR HAND

WITH ALL THIS YOU TAKE THE TIME
TO LISTEN TO A CHILD'S CRY
YOU STOP AND LEAN AND BEND AN EAR
WHENEVER ONE OF YOUR OWN DRAWS NEAR

CHILDREN'S SONGS

THROUGH CHILDREN'S SONGS THE OLD SET FREE
HIDDEN TRUTHS NOW PLAIN TO SEE
SIMPLE TRUTHS OF NURSERY RHYMES
MISSED BY THE OLD SO MANY TIMES

THEOLOGIAN'S WORDS SO GREAT AND GRAND
MADE SIMPLE IN THE CHILD'S HAND
THE SIMPLE TRUTH THE CHILD SEES
THE FATHER GAVE HIS SON FOR ME

THICK BOOKS BIG WORDS TRY TO EXPLAIN
AND COMFORT IN THE TIME OF PAIN
BUT NOW I SING THIS LITTLE SONG
LITTLE ONES TO HIM BELONG,
I AM WEAK BUT HE IS STRONG

TRUTH BE KNOWN WE ALL MUST SEE
WE ALL ARE LITTLE JUST LIKE ME
SO WHEN IN TROUBLE, DRED, OR FEAR
YOU NEED TO FEEL THE SAVIOR NEAR
SING THE SONGS, YOU KNOW THE ONES
AND YOU WILL SEE THE BATTLE WON

THE FAMILY

FAMILY PRAYER

OUR FATHER IN HEAVEN
    YOURS AND MINE "OUR" SAYS TO ME
    WE ARE JOINED AS FAMILY
    FATHER SPEAKS OF OWNERSHIP AND LOVE
    HEAVEN AUTHORITY FROM ABOVE

HOLLOWED BE YOUR NAME
    SPOKE WITH HOLY HUSH HIS NAME SHOULD BE
    NEVER LIGHTLY BY YOU OR ME
    FATHER FORGIVE ME WHEN IN STRESS
    I MISUSE THE NAME I LOVE BEST

YOUR KINGDOM COME
    WITHIN, WITHOUT MY PRAYER WILL BE
    YOUR KINGDOM TO HAVE ITS RULE IN ME
    THEN SPREAD IT WIDE MY WILL BE MY GOAL
    FOR YOUR KINGDOM TO GIVE MY ALL

YOUR WILL BE DONE ON EARTH AS IN HEAVEN
    THERE'S NO DEBATE OR ARGUMENT
    IN HEAVEN WHEN YOUR WORD IS SENT
    MAY IT BE THE SAME WITHIN MY HEART
    WITHOUT QUESTION TO DO MY PART

GIVE US THIS DAY OUR DAILY BREAD
    MY SPIRIT, SOUL, AND BODY IN YOUR HAND
    I TRUST YOU TO FULFILL YOUR PLAN
    TO KEEP ME FIT SO I CAN DO
    EVERY TASK THAT COMES FROM YOU

FORGIVE OUR DEBTS AS WE FORGIVE OUR DEBTORS
    IN LOVE FORGIVE THE DEBTS OWED ME
    LIKE MY SAVIOR THE DEBTS OWED THEE
    TRUE LIFE AND FREEDOM I WILL FIND
    IF I KEEP THIS TRUTH IN MIND

LEAD US NOT INTO TEMPTATION
    I'LL TRUST IN YOU AS I TREAD
    EVEN IN THE DARK AND DREAD
    FOR YOU KNOW THAT I AM BUT DUST
    SO I WILL TRUST YOU, I MUST, I MUST

DELIVER US FROM THE EVIL ONE
    LIKE GOLIATH MY FOE STANDS TALL
    AND LIKE DAVID I AM SMALL
    SO LIKE DAVID I'LL TRUST GOD'S MIGHT
    GUARANTEED TO WIN THE FIGHT

FOR THINE IS THE KINGDOM AND THE POWER AND THE GLORY FOREVER

    YOU ALONE ARE WORTHY TO BE KING
    ALL THE POWER IS IN THEE
    ALL GLORY IS TO YOU ALONE
    SEATED ON THE ETERNAL THRONE

AMEN

    FOR THOUSANDS OF YEARS THIS PRAYER'S BEEN SAID
    KNOWN BY HEART BUT STAYED IN HEAD
    BUT HERE IN FAITH LET IT BE KNOWN
    AMEN, AMEN IT SHALL BE SO

MY ETERNAL FAMILY

I ONCE LAID IN ASHES
UNTIL JESUS CAME ALONG
PICKED ME UP CLEANSED MY SOUL
AND GAVE ME A PLACE WHERE I BELONG

NOW I'M IN A FAMILY
OF PEOPLE JUST LIKE ME
LOST IN SIN AND BONDAGE
TILL JESUS SET US FREE

WHAT PEACE AND JOY FILL THIS HOUSE
THIS HOME IS FILLED WITH SONG
THIS PLACE OF LOVE AND SAFETY
IS THE PLACE THAT I BELONG

FROM NOW AND THROUGH ETERNITY
THIS IS THE PLACE FOR ME
JUST AS I AM AND PERFECTING
MY ETERNAL FAMILY

FAMILY AT HOME

LIKE A FAMILY AT HOME
IN HOUSE WARM AND TIGHT
BEFORE A COZY FIRE
ON A COLD AND SNOWY NIGHT

WE LAUGH AND CRY AND SOMETINES FIGHT
LIKE FAMILIES DO WRONG OR RIGHT
BUT OUR FATHER'S THERE TO RESTORE
RELATIONSHIPS AND HEARTS THAT ARE TORN

NOT PERFECT YET BUT WE WILL BE
WHEN TOGETHER IN ETERNITY
HERE TOGHETHER WE'LL STRUGGLE ON
HAND IN HAND ARM IN ARM

MESS WITH ONE YOU MESS WITH ALL
WE RALLY TO THE ONE WHO CALLS
TO THE DEATH IT MAY BE
MY BROTHER DID IT FOR YOU AND ME

SO BROTHER AND SISTER COME TO THE MEAL
THE RESERVATIONS MADE YOUR PLACE IS SET
YOU BELONG THERE'S NO REGRET
FOR OUR SAVIOR PAID THE DEBT

HOW TO BAKE

LIKE DAUGHTER IN THE KITCHEN HELPING MOMMY BAKE
WORKING TOGETHER TO MAKE A TASTY CAKE
FASTER EASIER IT WOULD BE TO DO IT ON HER OWN
BUT THE PLAN THAT MOMMY HAS IS TO HELP THE DAUGHTER GROW

LIKE A SON IN THE SHOP WITH FATHER CLOSE AT HAND
WITH LOVE AND PATIENCE A WOODEN TOY TO MAKE
THE FATHER COULD DO IT FASTER AND WITHOUT MISTAKE
BUT THE FATHER PLANS A MIGHTY MAN TO MAKE

DO YOU SEE WHAT IS MEANT BY THIS LITTLE POEM
OUR GOD COULD DO IT ALL AND BETTER ON HIS OWN
BUT OUT OF LOVE AND DESIRE FOR FELLOWSHIP AND GROWTH
HE INCLUDES US IN HIS WONDROUS PLAN

SO DON'T BE PUFFED UP WHEN IN VICTORY YOU STAND
OR DEFEATED WHEN IT SEEMS YOU'VE MISSED HIS PLAN
YOUR GOD HAS A PLAN BEYOND YOUR GRASP
SO LOOK TO HIM AND TRUST IN HIS GUIDING HAND

WHY

WHY SHOULD I FEEL SO BOUND UP
WHEN HE'S PROMISED TO SET ME FREE
WHY IS MY HEART NOT JOYFUL
SINCE HE'S PLEDGED HIS LOVE FOR ME

LIFE DOWN HERE CAN BE A DRAG
WEIGHED DOWN BY WOES AND CARES
LIKE SOGGY CLOTHES WEIGHING DOWN
A TIRED DROWNING MAN

SO I WILL LOOK UP TO THE ONE THE SPARROWS TRUST FOR FOOD
KNOWING THAT I'M WORTH MUCH MORE THAT WILL LIFT MY MOOD
SO I'LL SOAR LIKE THAT BIRD UP TO THE ONE ABOVE
WHO CARES WHAT HAPPENS DOWN BELOW I'M WITH THE ONE I LOVE

I THINK OF HIS CREATION EVERYTHING HE'S MADE
REMEMBERING THAT MAN'S THE ONLY ONE THE CREATOR DIED TO SAVE
WHAT JOY AND WONDER FILL MY SOUL WHEN STOP TO THINK
THE HOLY ONE WHO MADE IT ALL LOVES AND CARES FOR ME

ON MY OWN

ON MY OWN I WILL BE
ALONE I'LL WIN THE VICTORY
THAT'S THE LIE WITHIN MY SOUL
THAT'S WHY I END UP IN A HOLE

YOU'RE REALLY NOT ALONE HE SAYS
I AM HERE TO LIFT YOUR HEAD
DON'T BE DISCOURAGED WHEN YOU FALL
IT'S NOT THE END IF YOU CALL

I'M WAITING HERE TO LEND A HAND
COME TO ME I HAVE A PLAN
THE VICTORY IS WITH ME AND YOU
DEEP INSIDE YOU KNOW IT'S TRUE

SO WITH HIM I WILL WALK
IF IN DISTRESS WITH HIM I'LL TALK
WHEN IN FEAR TO HIM I'LL GO
FOREVERMORE NOT ON MY OWN

NIGHT SONG

SIMPLE SONG IN THE NIGHT
SEARCHING LOOKING FOR A LIGHT
VERSES PENNED FROM LONG AGO
SPEAK TO THE HEART WHERE TO GO

THE HEART FINDS HOPE IN WORDS OF OLD
REMIND OF FAITHS STORIES TOLD
THEN AS HOPE GIVES BIRTH TO FAITH
WE KNOW THAT GOD WILL MAKE A WAY

SO AS WE SING THESE HYMNS OF OLD
VOLUME INCREASE FAITH IS BOLD
THEN WE SHOUT FOR ALL TO HEAR
VICTORY, VICTORY THE LORD IS HERE

REALITY

REALITY WE TRUST IN AND WALK IN DAY BY DAY
EXPERIENCED THROUGH SENSES TO GUIDE US ON OUR WAY
KNOWLEDGE GAINED THROUGH SENSES SIGHT AND SMELL AND TOUCH
CAN BE LIKE LOOKING THROUGH A FOG, LIMITED AT BEST

BUT THERE IS ANOTHER REALM THOUGH IT CAN'T BE SEEN
MORE POWERFUL AND REAL THAN OUR REALITY
THE REALITY THAT CAN'T BE SEEN GOVERNS THE ONE THAT CAN
GOVERNED WITH WISDOM BY AN UNSEEN HAND

THE REALITY I SPEAK OF IS THE ONE OF GOD HIS OWN
MORE REAL THAN WE COULD EVER KNOW THOUGH IT CAN'T BE SHOWN
THOUGH IT SEAMS A MYSTERY TO OUR MINDS IT'S TRUE
STILL EVERY TIME WE TOUCH IT WE KNOW IT, WE JUST DO

SO IN YOUR STRIFE AND GROPING IN THIS REALITY
KNOW THAT THERE'S A BIGGER REALM THE ONE YOU CANNOT SEE
TRUST IN THE ONE WHO HOLDS IT ALL IN HIS MIGHTY HAND
HE LOVES YOU AND YOU'RE A PART OF HIS ETERNAL PLAN

I AM

OCEAN DEEP OR MOUNTAIN PEAK
I'LL BE THERE I NEVER SLEEP
DARK OF NIGHT OR BRIGHT OF DAY
TRUST IN ME I AM THE WAY

QUESTIONS DEEP RUN THROUGH YOUR MIND
BUMPING INTO THINGS LIKE THE BLIND
YOU SEARCH FOR ANSWERS YOUR SOUL TO SOOTH
LOOK TO ME I AM THE TRUTH

LOOKING FOR A WAY TO LIVE
MORE THAN JUST THE TAKE AND GIVE
MORE THAN WORK, STRAIN, AND STRIFE
COME TO ME I AM THE LIFE

ALL YOU NEED IS FOUND IN ME
IT IS THAT SIMPLE JUST BELIEVE
ON THE CROSS I DID MY PART
WAITING FOR YOU TO GIVE YOUR HEART

LIKE MY SAVIOR

LIKE MY SAVIOR I WOULD BE
GIVING LIFE TO ALL I SEE
BRING LIFE TO THOSE IN DEATH
BRINGING TO THE WEARY REST

BUT I CAN'T PAY THE PRICE HE PAID
THE MANY STRIPES ON HIM WERE LAID
UNTIL AT LAST UPON THE CROSS
HE GAVE HIS LIFE TO SAVE THE LOST

I CANNOT DIE FOR SOMEONE'S SIN
OR BEAR THERE BURDEN DEEP WITHIN
IS THERE A CROSS THAT I MUST BEAR
TO BRING YOUR SALVATION TO THE LOST

YOU WERE REJECTED, DESPISED, AND SPURNED
FROM THIS PICTURE I SHOULD LEARN
IT COULD BE THE SAME FOR ME
THE COST I PAY THE LOST SET FREE

THE BATTLE

COME SONS

COME ALL SONS FROM EAST AND WEST
NORTH AND SOUTH HIS CHOSEN BEST
COME WITH ARMOR COME WITH SHIELD
COME WITH TRUSTY SWORD TO WIELD

FEAR NOT THE FOE OR HIS JESTS
THOUGH HE WILL TRY AND DO HIS BEST
IT MATTERS NOT WHAT HE MAY DO OR SAY
CHRIST SAID IT ALL ON RESURRECTION DAY

ON THAT DAY DEATH WAS DEAD
JESUS CRUSHED THE SERPENT'S HEAD
SO TO THE BATTLE WE CAN RUN
IN CONFIDENCE THE BATTLE'S WON

MOUNTAIN TOP VIEW

KEEP ON WALKING DO NOT STOP
TILL YOU REACH THE MOUNTAIN TOP
YOU'VE COME FAR, BUT THERE'S MORE TO GO
SOMETIMES FAST SOMETIMES SLOW

THERE WILL BE TIMES OF NEED REST
TIMES OF REFRESHING BY QUIET BROOK
IN COOL SHADE YOU CAN STAY
WELL CONTEMPLATE THE COMING DAY

THEN OFF WE'LL GO, I'LL LEAD THE WAY
SOMETIMES AT NIGHT, SOMETIMES AT DAY
KNOWING THAT I AM THE LIGHT
NO MATTER WHAT THE PATH IS BRIGHT

I'LL GIVE YOU STRENGTH TO SEE IT THROUGH
WHEN EXHAUSTED I'LL CARRY YOU
I AM THE LORD I CANNOT FAIL
NO MATTER HOW HIGH OR STEEP THE TRAIL

SO COME WITH ME DON'T BE AFRAID
I AM THE LORD, MY PLAIN IS MADE
THE VERY PLAN THAT BEARS YOUR NAME
I AM THE LORD I DO NOT CHANGE

I'VE MADE MY CHOICE YOU ARE THE ONE
YOU ARE MY DAUGHTER OR MY SON
YOU'LL BE ASTONISHED, THE VIEW YOU'LL SEE
ON THE MOUNTAIN TOP WITH ME

SON OF MINE

SON OF MINE
BEFORE TIME
CHOSEN WITH CHEER
I DRAW YOU NEAR

PRICE WAS PAID
DEAL WAS MADE
IT IS DONE
YOU ARE MY SON

FROM NOW ON THE UPWARD PATH
LOVE, ENCOURAGEMENT NO WRATH
SO COME AND SEE WHAT CAN BE
ALL THAT YOU CAN BE THROUGH ME

AMAZED AND JOYFUL YOU WILL BE
IF YOU KEEP IN STEP WITH ME
YOU CAN DO IT I KNOW YOU CAN
FOR I'VE MADE YOU A MIGHTY MAN

SO RUN WITH ME WE'LL SCALE THE HEIGHTS
THE ENEMY WE'LL PUT TO FLIGHT
WITH MY ARMY CLOTHED IN WHITE
SWIFT AND SURE WITH ARMOR BRIGHT

THEN IN GLORY WE WILL STAND
WITH OUR FATHER HAND IN HAND
GIVING GLORY TO THE SON
AND THE SPIRIT THREE IN ONE

I WILL NOT YIELD

FEAR, DEPRESSION, FEELING LOW
DON'T WANT TO LET THE FEELINGS GROW
SO I RUN AS FAST AS I CAN GO
UNTIL SOMETHING INSIDE SHOUTS NO

THIS IS NOT THE WAY TO FIGHT
MY GOD HAS GIVEN ME THE MIGHT
WITH TRUTH AND FAITH I'LL MAKE MY STAND
I WILL NOT YIELD AN INCH OF LAND

THE CROSS OF CHRIST HAS CUT THE BANDS
SO NOW WITH WEAPONS IN MY HANDS
I'LL SWING THE SLING AND TAKE MY SHOT
AND STAND VICTORIOUS ON THE MOUNTAIN TOP

POWER LOVE

POWER, POWER, POWER
LOVE, LOVE, LOVE
POWER, POWER, POWER
LOVE FROM ABOVE

MANY A FROZEN HEART
LIKE BUTTER ON A PLATE
WILL RESIST THE HAMMERS BLOWS
BUT YIELD TO BURNING KNIFE

THE LOVE OF GOD IS LIKE BURNING KNIFE
THAT MELTS THE FROZEN MASS
BUT THERE IS HEALING AND RESTORATION
ALWAYS IN ITS PATH

THE VICTORY

WHEN THE RACE IS RUN

FAITHFUL THROUGH THE AGES
AND IN MY LIFE AS WELL
IN THE WIND-SWEPT STORMY SEAS
AND IN THE OCEAN SWELL

ALWAYS THERE AT TIMES UNSEEN
A COMFORT IN THE DARK
SAFE IN TRUSTING THE LORD MY GOD
LIKE NOAH IN THE ARK

BY HIM THE FOOLISH CONFOUND THE WISE
THE ONE WHO'S TALES I TELL
ALSO MAKES THE WEAK SO STRONG
TO STORM THE GATES OF HELL

AND WHEN THE RACE IS RUN
I'M GONNA BE IN THAT NUMBER
NO ONE HUMBLER
WHEN THE SAINTS GO MARCHIN' IN

WHAT WILL WE SEE

WHAT WILL WE SEE WHEN AT LAST THIS LIFE IS AT ITS END
WHAT IS IN STORE FOR US AROUND THE FINAL BEND
WE TALK AND JOKE ABOUT IT TO EASE THE FEAR WITHIN
WILL IT BE JUST BETTER HERE OR WAY BEYOND OUR THOUGHT

WILL WE FLOAT ON CLOUDS OF WHITE
WHEN OUR LIFE ON EARTH IS DONE
PLAYING GOLF WOULD BE FUN
I'LL FINALLY GET A HOLE-IN-ONE

WE READ ABOUT HEAVEN IN THE BIBLE AND OTHER BOOKS
IT SEEMS THE MODERN CONCEPT IS NOT THE WAY IT LOOKS
I AM NOT THE CENTER GOD IS ON THE THRONE
AND WE ARE THERE IN JOYFUL WORSHIP OF THE ONE WHO BROUGHT US HOME

THE BIBLE SPEAKS IN PICTURES OF THE SCENES ABOVE
BUT I KNOW THAT I WILL BE IN THE ARMS OF LOVE
NO SIN OR TEARS OR PAIN WILL YOU FIND UP THERE
IN THE SCENES OF GLORY NO ONE HAS A CARE

HEAVEN IS TOO BIG AND GRAND FOR MY MIND TO GRASP
BEYOND ALL IMAGINATION FOUND WITHIN MY HEART
SO I WILL PONDER WHAT I'LL SEE LET MY HEART RUN WILD
KNOWING THAT THE BEST I DO COMPARED WILL BE MILD

HEAVENLY CROWN

I AM THE LORD I DO NOT CHANGE
MY PLANS ARE NEVER REARRANGED
MY CALL ON YOU REMAINS THE SAME
FROM DAY ONE UNTIL TODAY

UP AND DOWN, LEFT AND RIGHT
OPENED WIDE THEN CLOSED TIGHT
I'M IN CONTROL I HAVE THE WHEEL
EVERYTHING OPPOSED MUST YIELD

TAKE COMFORT IN THE PLAN I'VE MADE
IN ETERNITY IT'S LAID
I NEVER FAIL IN WHAT I'VE SAID
TO PLACE THE CROWN UPON YOUR HEAD

CPSIA information can be obtained
at www.ICGtesting.com
Printed in the USA
BVHW030928230223
659068BV00005B/160